Pim? Pim?

By Sally Cowan

Sim is at the tap.

Is Pim at the tap?

It is Pip.

Pip sips at the tap.

Sim is at the pit.

Is it Pim?

It is Tam.

Tam sits at the pit.

Sim sat.

It is Pim.

CHECKING FOR MEANING

1. Who is looking for Pim? *(Literal)*

2. What is Tam doing at the pit? *(Literal)*

3. Why do you think Sim wanted to find Pim? *(Inferential)*

EXTENDING VOCABULARY

Pim	Look at the word *Pim*. How many sounds are in the word? What other words can you think of that rhyme with *Pim*?
tap	Look at the word *tap*. What word would you make if you add an *s* to the end of *tap*? How would this change the meaning?
pit	What sort of pit is Tam sitting at? What other types of pits do you know of?

MOVING BEYOND THE TEXT

1. Birds live in nests. What other sorts of homes can animals live in?

2. What do you think Sim and Pim eat?

3. Where would you look if you wanted to find one of your friends at school?

4. Where could you hide if you were playing hide-and-seek at home or at school?

SPEED SOUNDS

| Mm | Ss | Aa | Pp | Ii | Tt |

PRACTICE WORDS

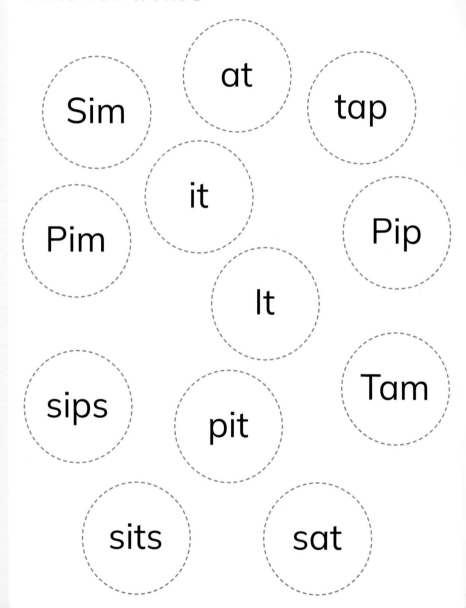

Sim

at

tap

it

Pim

Pip

It

sips

Tam

pit

sits

sat